Selfless and Heartless Pursuits

Selfless and Heartless Pursuits

stories about 4 animals, birds and the moon
for the reflection of families, children and students

JONATHAN F AWASOM

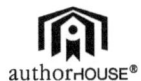

authorHOUSE®

AuthorHouse™ LLC
1663 Liberty Drive
Bloomington, IN 47403
www.authorhouse.com
Phone: 1-800-839-8640

The author of this book can be reached at :
Email: Jonathan_light2000@yahoo.com
Phone: 201-878-5829

Published by AuthorHouse 08/08/2014

ISBN: 978-1-4969-2450-6 (sc)
ISBN: 978-1-4969-2449-0 (e)

Library of Congress Control Number: 2014911947

Contents

Dedication

This book is dedicated to the loving and eternal memory of my grandparents, Tata Nicodemus Nde Awasom and Nimo Swirinkwi Elizabeth Awasom, the oral historians of our family. They were devoted followers of Jesus Christ who were guided by the Christian principles and African traditional values they learned orally, and they handed down those principles and values to their grandchildren through the same oral tradition. Through their exemplary lives of selfless love and sacrifice they saw to it that their grandchildren received an education of both the head and heart.

Acknowledgement

It is not easy to write an acknowledgement to include everyone but here I have tried to be realistic to say "thank you" to individuals and people who have impacted my life in myriad of ways.

I would like to sincerely thank Christine Orzepowski for her devotion and help in editing this book and especially for the final stage in proof reading. Her expertise as a retired English teacher was very useful and I am so thankful to Christine for her input.

By the same token, I am grateful to my friends for their financial support towards the publication of this book. I could not have done this work without their support. I am particularly grateful to Ms Catherine Mary Mbu and Victoria Herzberg for their help.

Thank you my friend Giddy Ticha, Emily Muelken, Evelyn Meva, Mercy Yayuh, Ifeyinywa Lilian Okafor, Renae Baker, Rosie and David, Bob Ritter, John Weidermann, Rev. Victor O Anjorin , John and Sally Morris, Deshonda Renfro, Dr.Jean-Bosco Tagne, Nancy Mma, Rev. Dr. Kenneth Numfor, Chum Ignatius , Sally Kum, Musoro Olive, Brother Paul Ngongang, Fai Robert and Charity Mbatia. Friends are like little stars in the sky of our journeys. They shine on us and provide light that guide our path. They cheer us up. They critique us. They praise us. They make us laugh .They check on us. They think about us. They share with us. They are friends for a purpose because they love us, anyways. Irene Achebodt Tancho,Edith Achebodt,Rachael Achebodt,Daniel Achebodt,Belinda Achebodt,Faith Achebodt,Pa and Ma Achebodt,Hon. Pa and Ma Ogork Ntui, Pafe Njike and Jacky Nungu.

And to all of you, my awesome teachers and friends from elementary school through university in Cameroon and the United States, you have been my encouragers. You believed in me and some of you always asked me, "When are you going to start publishing?" Well, this is for you!

I am also profoundly indebted to Prof. Indira Junghare, University of Minnesota. To me she is a perfect embodiment of the human spirit I have ever met in my life. As the President and Founder of Diversity, Ethics and Peace (DEP). I was truly inspired by her leadership, mentorship, kindness and passion towards fostering a diverse human family where people are living in peace and harmony with a sense of ethical responsibility.

Indeed, Dick and Londa Amundson, you are a special couple. Although you have been out of sight, you have not been out of my mind. I thank you and my young friends during our 40 days wilderness experience. I will never forget our Tentmakers Young Leaders training. I am grateful for the opportunity you provided me through your ministries and friends to be part of such a novel idea whose time was ripe for us.

I cannot forget to recognize Denis Brown and Bryant Berry with their families at Christ Presbyterian Church, Edina Minnesota for their love, friendship and support while I was in Minnesota.

Hello Shirley Engelmeier, Ross , John Michael and Zack. You are all evergreen in my memory during my stay in Minnesota. Shirley you espouse the notion of inclusion in theory and practice. I am one damn lucky person who captured your spirit of inclusive humanity from Seminary to Golden Valley.

Yes, I am a Christian and my Christian brothers and sisters in the Lord have a special place in my heart for inspiring and training me with the spirit of servant leadership that has shaped my commitment to being a voice for the voiceless under oppression and injustice.

They include my Christian friends of Presbyterian Church, Bastos, Presbyterian Church Etoug-egbe, Presbyterian Church CCAST Complex Chaplaincy and Presbyterian Church Baforkum all in Cameroon. In the United States, I thank Christ Presbyterian Church Edina Minnesota, Westminster Presbyterian Church Minneapolis, Tentmakers Young Leaders Ministries, Minnesota ,Spirit Garage Church Minneapolis, Christ Embassy Church Newark New Jersey, First Presbyterian Church Peachtree City Atlanta Georgia, Presbyterian Church of Upper Montclair, New Jersey, Bethlehem Baptist Church Newark, New Jersey, Metropolitan Baptist Church Newark, New Jersey and Foursquare Church Orange, New Jersey for their love, friendship and support in my faith journey. You all inspired me with your beautiful smiles and kind hearts at different levels we interacted as God's family. I always feel privileged and blessed to know you.

Lastly, thank you to my amazing colleagues at work and also child sponsors during the World Vision Child sponsorship campaign at One Garden State Plaza Mall in New Jersey. I will never forget you, ladies and gentlemen, for your sacrifice, humility, team spirit, loyalty, courage and passionate commitment to help change the lives of children afflicted by intolerance, violent conflicts, poverty and injustice around the world. Your enthusiasm and compassion was infectious and much appreciated. Of. Course, thank you so much World Vision for the platform you have given us to make a difference on the lives of these children.

Thanks to my beloved family, far and near for your thoughtfulness, prayers, phone calls and kind words during life time challenges.

I love you all and thank you, thank you for embracing one another.

Jonathan

Selfless and Heartless Pursuits:
stories about 4 animals, birds and the moon for reflection of families, children and students

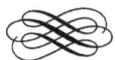

"Selfless and Heartless Pursuits" consists of four morale fables from Cameroon, Africa, whose characters are the animals, the birds and the moon impersonating human beings from all walks of life who are bound together by challenging circumstances.

The tension between selfless and heartless pursuits reminds us that we need to cultivate a spirit of effective communication and selfless love which are the lights that shine within us as we work to overcome the darkness of bullying, abuse, violation, oppression and injustice in our societies.

When I thought about writing these stories, I was thinking about how we should continue to break down barriers and build bridges across cultures. But most importantly, my desire to empower families, children, students, community leaders, religious leaders and public officials to reflect on the virtue of selfless love and the vice of heartless pursuit.

My grandparents who did not read or write were wonderful story tellers. Every single day of my life, these stories bring back good memories of fun and entertainment during the days I and my siblings spent with our grandparents. I spent the most inspiring and entertaining moments of my childhood with them as they narrated these stories as a way of orally educating their grandchildren to cultivate good manners, moral values and wisdom in making personal decisions.

These moral fables are an invitation to us to treat one another with respect and dignity. More importantly, the fables challenge us to live in peace and harmony with our neighbors because "an eye for an eye" may not be the best way to resolve a conflict. How well can one seek justice without vengeance? How do we draw the line between exacting justice so that it does not spill over into vengeance?

Some of these stories teach us about our personal space and privacy and also about our rights, responsibility and accountability in our world of immense cross-cultural diversity. The powerful application of wisdom in problem solving by weak and unarmed ones also stands out in these stories. Is there an alternative path to conflict resolution other than getting even and what are the consequences of our actions? Can we forgive where forgiveness is called for? Does the ability to take ownership of our faults help in our growth and transformation to become selfless in life?

I am always challenged by these stories and perhaps you feel the same, too. It is my hope that you take a moment to explore these stories and enjoy the humor as well as learn from the wisdom and knowledge that they are intended for. To be very realistic, every situation of conflict in this life has forced me to use these stories as a mirror for deep reflection. What is the cost of indulging into a conflict? Is it worthless or it is worthwhile to be involved? Have you ever started a conflict or blamed for being responsible for a conflict?

We human beings are still making the same mistakes because we might have different pursuits in life other than selfless love. Whichever path we choose in this life, we must remember, it will define us and our relationships with one another for a lifetime. Therefore, we must be mindful of our pursuits in life. The question for each of us is, what defines you, selfless pursuit or heartless pursuit?

Thank you

Jonathan Awasom

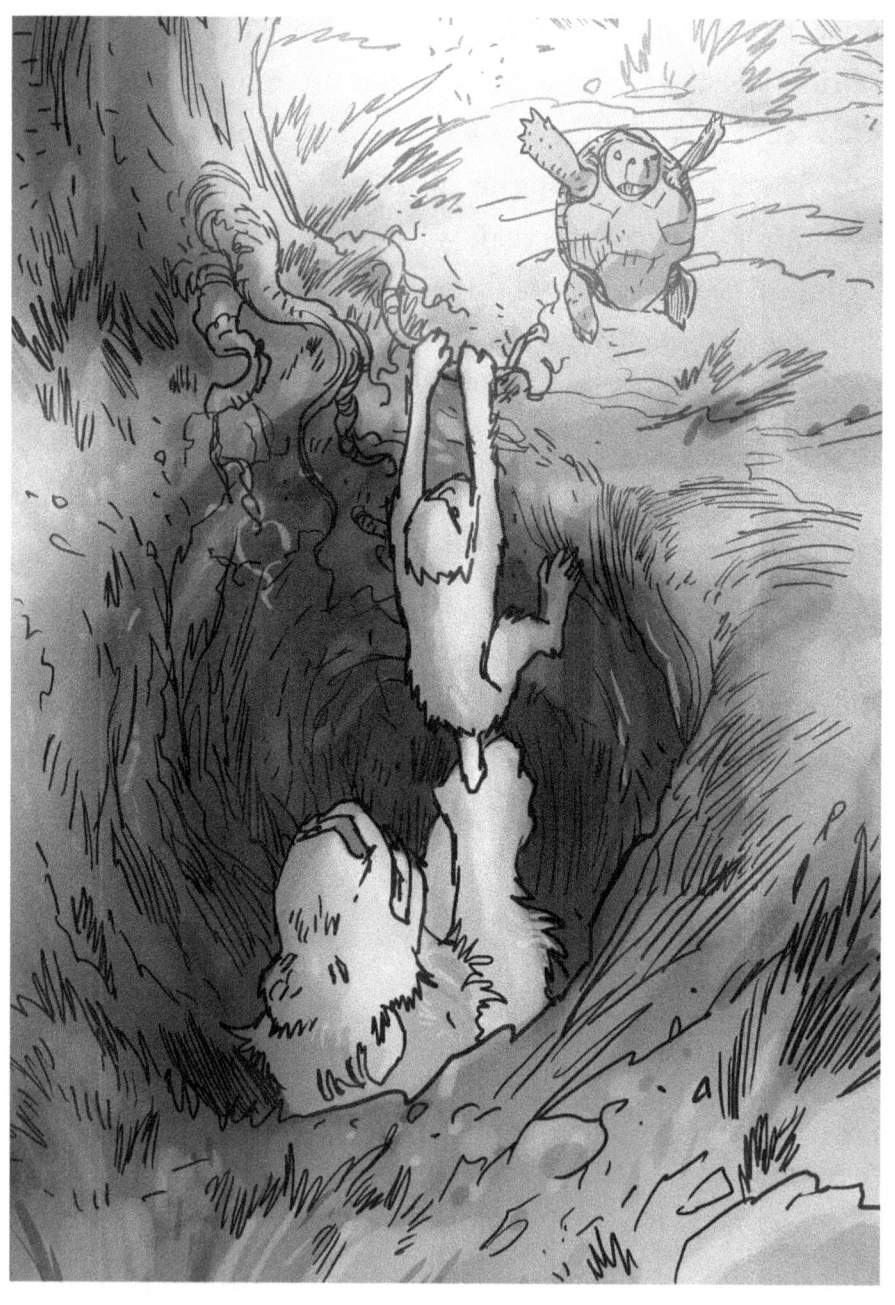

The Lion King of the Jungle Falls into His Own Trap

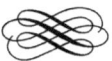

"The Lion, King of the Jungle" is a very familiar phrase. The Lion is in charge there but must share the habitat that is under his control with other animals like the Monkey and the Tortoise. But every other animal in the jungle is bound to be afraid of the Lion because of his past harmful activities of preying upon the small animals and those who crossed his path.

This is the main reason why every animal is afraid of him, including human beings. Consequently, the Lion is always living in isolation. When he is lying low, it means he is not hungry, but once he is in action and walking up and down the jungle from one place to the other, it means he is hungry and desperately hunting for his next meal.

Whoever comes across his path must be attacked by the angry, hungry Lion. But as fate would have it, on one fateful day, the Lion

King of the Jungle had completely ignored the fact that outside of the jungle lived humans.

These human beings were equally involved in shaping their own environment to be suitable and habitable for them. On one occasion, while hunting and farming a human left an unfinished well he was digging in the jungle. As it happened, while wandering around the Lion King fell into the well. At that juncture, he was trapped inside.

Initially, it did not occur to the Lion that he was in deep trouble, but soon after several unsuccessful attempts, he could not immediately come out of the hole. He tried to jump but failed to climb to safety. He tried to hold the walls of the hole but he had no ability to climb, and before long he was trapped inside the hole for 48 hours. He was not only afraid but very hungry.

Before he fell into the hole, he was already quite hungry, which meant now his situation was becoming very critical. Being tired and suffering from fatigue, the Lion began to cry out for help! He roared and roared desperately at the top of his voice, but the animals were afraid of him and thought it was his trick.

It was not long after when things took a different turn. The Monkey, who was hopping from one branch to the other, spotted the Lion inside the hole after hearing his loud and desperate outcry! The Monkey made his way to the hole and behold he saw The Lion King of the Jungle gasping for breath and looking humble and desperate.

"Oh my gosh! What happened to you sir?" cried the monkey.

The Lion said," I was taking a walk to make sure that things were under my control when I fell into this hole dug by those cruel humans. I am so upset. I have tried to get out but I can't make it. Can you help me? I can't see clearly; are you the Monkey? Please, I need your help. I will be very grateful for your kindness. Do whatever it takes to help me."

"Hmmm," thought the Monkey, "Yes, I am the Monkey, but I don't know how to help you! I am afraid that you might hurt me because you are notorious for that. Besides, I am alone and no other animal in this jungle even knows you have fallen and are unable to rescue yourself. They might just want you to remain inside the hole!"

The Lion pleaded, "Please, you know I can't hurt you. I never even met you since you live on the tree branches and are always jumping from one branch to the other. I am not going to hurt you. Promise me that you will help get me out. Please, help me!"

The Monkey said, "Ok, let me think! How can I help you since I don't have the tools like humans have? If I call the attention of humans, I am not sure they would like to help because everyone seems to be afraid of you because you might devour them.

I really feel for you. The only thing I have now is my long tail. I am going to stoop down by the hole and send my tail all the way down for you to hold onto it. In that way, I will pull you out while holding onto the roots of the tree just by the hole. Are you ready to jump and catch my tail?"

The Lion grumbled, "Ok, I will jump and hold your tail, but are you serious? Can you really help me with your tail? ''

The Monkey responded, "Yes, with my tail; everything is under my control."

"Ok," the Lion agreed. "Thank you so much for being willing to help me."

Once an agreement was reached to begin, the rescue mission was undertaken by the Monkey. He took a position and held on to the roots of a tree that was growing by the hole the Lion had fallen into. He then lowered his tail into the hole and slipped it all the way down to about seven feet. The monkey was quite strong and had a very long tail, too.

It was easy for the lion to jump and hold unto the Monkey's tail as the Monkey anchored his back feet into the soil and simultaneously held the roots of the tree with his front legs that worked magically like a crane or pulley. This bold action of the Monkey alone enabled the Lion to be pulled out of the hole.

What an amazing feat of strength was just executed by the monkey! One good turn deserves another! But now there was a twist of events. Once the Lion was rescued and he became free again, he did not want to let go of the Monkey. A quarrel erupted between them.

The Monkey was smiling and excited and said to the Lion," Wow, you made it out safely! I am happy you are now free again. I have to go because I did not plan to stop here. My family is waiting for me so that we can have dinner together."

The Lion, while staring at the Monkey with his angry looks said, "Let me think. Hmmmmm, you want to leave me here alone, but what am I going to eat now? I am dying of hunger after having been in this hole for more than two days. Can I start by eating your tail?"

The Monkey was shocked and frightened. "What? You want to eat my tail after I rescued you? You should not pay me back with evil because if I did not come to your rescue, you would have suffered and died in that hole. So, please, let me go and I will look for food for you. You have to trust me because I have helped you."

As the quarrel became very intense, the tortoise, who could barely walk, happened to be nearby and overheard the Monkey and the Lion in this very tense disagreement. He noticed that the Monkey was fighting for his life. He crawled out from the nearby bush and showed up uninvited, as good neighbors do.

The Tortoise cleared his throat to signal his presence." Hummmm, gentlemen, what is happening that you are arguing? I had a very long day and I am very tired, too. I am sure you both are exhausted after a day's work."

"Oh no.We have some issues here and want to resolve them before it is too late, " protested the Lion.

The Monkey objected, "No, I did not have any issues with him until now! He fell into that hole and I came to his rescue, but now he does not want to let me go. He said he would kill me for food and I am terrified."

"Are you sure you rescued him?" asked the Tortoise. "How could you succeed in rescuing this large Lion from that hole? I can't believe this; it sounds like some kind of hoax. Monkey, are you trying to play games here? And you, Lion, you know I find it hard to believe this Monkey and I totally understand that some people are born to lie, but is it true that you were rescued from this hole?"

"Yes, he was very kind to me, but that was then! He owes me food because I am hungry. I just want to eat because I have been starved without food for more than two days! "cried the Lion.

"Ahhhhhh, I see. This is very interesting! "said the Tortoise. "This is really something! You expect me to believe that this small Monkey rescued you, the big Lion, from that hole all by himself without tools and help from the humans! Well, I want to see it first-hand. Prove that this is true. Jump back into the hole and let me watch the monkey perform the act again because nobody will ever believe this story. I think it is miraculous and amazing, and I will be your witness."

The Lion, King of the Jungle, was overwhelmed and carried away by the intrigues of the Tortoise. He had no idea that he was being set up. He took his hands off the tail of the Monkey and jumped back into the hole with the hope that the Monkey would repeat the same rescue action, this time with a witness present. But he was wrong. When the Lion jumped back into the hole, the Tortoise turned to the Monkey and ordered, "Leave immediately and never ever again come around here.Let the Lion stay in the hole."

The Monkey thanked the Tortoise and jumped onto the tree branches and dashed away while the tortoise simply disappeared slowly into the bush. The Lion remained trapped inside the hole for the second time and cried out for help unsuccessfully. Finally, he passed out and died of fatigue and hunger.

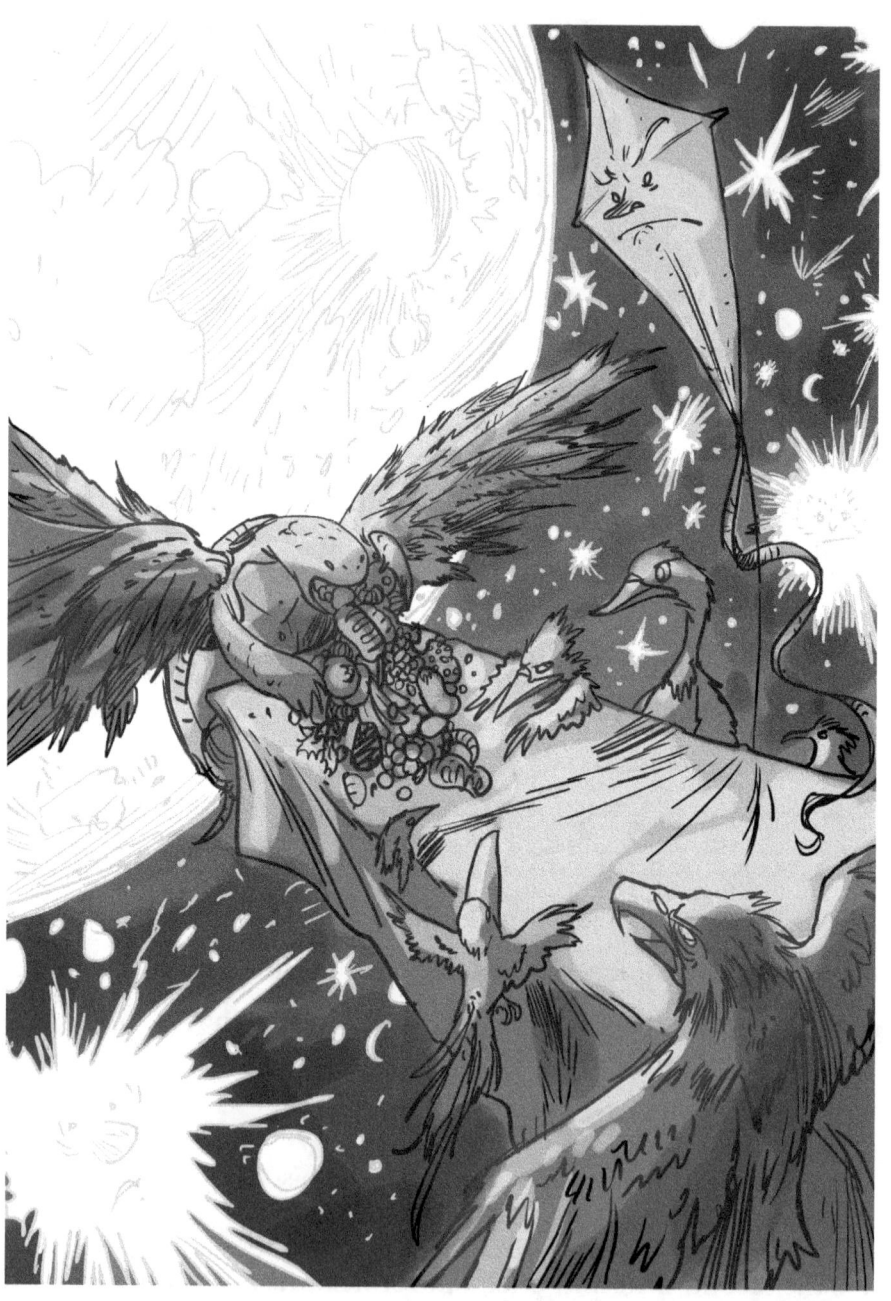

The Tortoise Tricked the Birds and the Moon

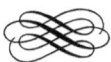

Treat others the way you would like to be treated

While human beings have learned to fly to the moon by rocket, birds by nature have always flown by themselves propelled to that height by their wings and the wind. It is obvious that the glamorous and exciting movement of the birds in the sky captured the imagination of humankind and inspired them to create aircraft.

Before astronauts ever went to the moon, the birds and the tortoise had been there at the pleasurable invitation of the moon. In fact, the first explorers to the moon were the birds and the tortoise. The birds resisted the force of gravity and navigated through the sky with freedom. The tortoise attempted to be like the birds but it never lasted.

As it happened, the moon had a birthday party many years ago. The moon wanted to celebrate her birthday with the company of friends from the earth. Over the years she felt that she had connected with the inhabitants of earth by shinning and giving light to them.

In fact, she wanted to close the gap that existed between her and the inhabitants of the earth as a result of their inability to fly to the Moon. So, for once in her life, she decided to invite some inhabitants from the earth to come and participate in her birthday party.

The Moon planned her party and invited the Stars and other inhabitants of the Sky. The invitation was sent to the earth only to the birds because they had wings and could fly to the Moon in defiance of the force of gravity. Literally, every other animal was disappointed because they could not fly to the Moon. Even humans who thought that they were the most intelligent and wise creatures, were not able to fly to the moon for this party. So, the birds were going to be the only honorable guests from the earth at the party.

At that juncture, the kite convened a general assembly of all the birds in the forest to plan their journey to the Moon. So they met on a tree in the forest nearby, to discuss the idea with the birds.

Meanwhile, the Tortoise was living in the forest, too and he overheard the birds planning to fly to the moon. He was interested because their discussions suggested that there would be a great deal of feasting and fun.

The Tortoise became jealous and so he began thinking of ways to join the birds on the moon, too. Then an idea came to his mind. He decided that he could ask each of the birds to donate a feather so that he would build two set of wings. In that way he would have the ability to fly like the birds. It sounded like a great idea.

So, after the birds separated from their meeting, the Hawk flew to search for food. Quickly the Tortoise appeared on site and coughed intentionally to seek the attention of the Hawk. Then he began inquiring about their meeting; the Hawk, who was really excited about it, gave him all the details. But the Tortoise stopped him and asked if he could go with the birds to the Moon. The Hawk laughed at him.

The Hawk expressed regret to the Tortoise and said, " I am sorry you can't come because you don't have wings to fly. No animal can come with us; sorry for that inconvenience."

"Please, wait a minute, I have an idea," said the Tortoise.

The Hawk was surprised and was eager to know what idea the Tortoise had and so he asked quickly, "Ok, Sir, what is your idea? Tell me because I need to go now."

The Tortoise said, "Well, I can fly to the Moon with you."

"How can you fly when you have no wings?" the Hawk laughed.

"Do you like my company and friendship?" asked the Tortoise.

"Of course, yes," said the Hawk. "I would like you to come; but it is not my fault that you don't have wings. Sorry, about that."

The Tortoise walked up to the Hawk and whispered into his ear, "I think each bird should lend me a feather. We can build two sets of wings and they would be inserted on my sides to enable me fly. I'd like to go because that will be quite an adventure. This will be our secret until we go to the Moon and return."

"I see what you mean," said the Hawk. "But it will be difficult because I don't know if the other birds will accept the idea to welcome you and also to sponsor you with their feathers. Anyway, I will do my best to present the matter in our next meeting two days from now. I have to run now. Thank you friend and I will let you know. Would you like to come to the meeting if you were invited? "

The Tortoise, while excited and smiling, said, "Yes, I will definitely honor the invitation if I am invited."

"Okay, I will let you know as soon as possible," said the Hawk, and then he flew away.

Eventually, the Tortoise was invited to the last planning meeting where he met with all the birds. The Kite chaired the meeting and by acclamation after all due consideration, each bird agreed to donate one of his feathers to the Tortoise.

The meeting ended with a closing remark from the Kite and he also officially welcomed the Tortoise into their company and said, "Our dear friend, on behalf of every bird here present, we are delighted to welcome you in our midst. Even though we are different, we are excited and pleased that through our imagination and creativity we have figured out a way for you to fly with us to this great party on the Moon. Now you have our feathers. You have inevitably become one of us. You are warmly welcome to fly with us to the Moon and we shall leave at sunset tomorrow. Have a good day and see you later."

Before the meeting came to a close, the Tortoise asked if he could speak. His request was granted. He thanked all the birds for giving him the opportunity but requested everyone to introduce himself for proper identification. So, all the other birds introduced themselves and when it was his turn, the Tortoise said since the Moon knew his name, he decided he would change his name for convenience.

While snickering he said, "My new name for this event is, "Forallofyou".The birds found that weird but did not know he had an ulterior motive for participating in the party.

Finally, the Tortoise and birds left for the Moon at sunset the following evening. It took them seven hours to arrive at the moon, at the time when the moon was shining and showing them the way. During the party, the food server brought food and treats, and placed them on the table in the room where the delegation from the earth was seated. Since she did not know their names individually, the server said, "This food is for all of you."

The birds knew that Forallofyou was the name of the Tortoise so each of them waited for their own food. While they waited indefinitely the Tortoise ate all by himself and become filled up and heavy. The birds became frustrated and disappointed. They felt humiliated by the Moon. Unfortunately, the Moon did not know that they were deprived of feasting.

They became even angrier because the Tortoise was greedy and ate everything that was brought to him. They began feeling that he was an intruder and regretted that they had invited him. They blamed the Hawk because he negotiated the deal between them and the Tortoise.

The Kite announced that they should leave immediately and fly back to the earth. The Hawk suggested that they should withdraw their feathers from the Tortoise before leaving. They all agreed unanimously. As they flew back to the earth, they each snatched their feathers from the Tortoise living him stranded on the

Moon. The last bird to leave was the Hawk. He expressed his disappointment with the Tortoise but still took his own feather.

Before the Hawk left, the Tortoise pleaded with him to tell his wife on earth to prepare a safe place for his landing at the courtyard. The Tortoise advised that she should build a comfortable platform with soft materials like sofas, mattresses, pillows and grass so that when he fell from the Moon, he would not break himself.

The Hawk flew to the earth and reported to the Tortoise's wife with a different story. The Hawk told her to gather all the broken bottles, bones, stones, logs of wood and pebble so that when the Tortoise fell from the Moon he would prove to the birds that he was tougher and stronger than they were.

The Hawk lied that it was a competition among them and that falling from the Moon was the last stage in the competition. Unfortunately, the Tortoise's wife heeded the orders from the Hawk. When she finally finished, the hawk flew back to the Moon and lied to the Tortoise by telling him that the safety platform was set. The Tortoise was convinced and immediately jumped from the Moon and fell on the hard surface and broke his shell into pieces. It was a tragic and painful end.

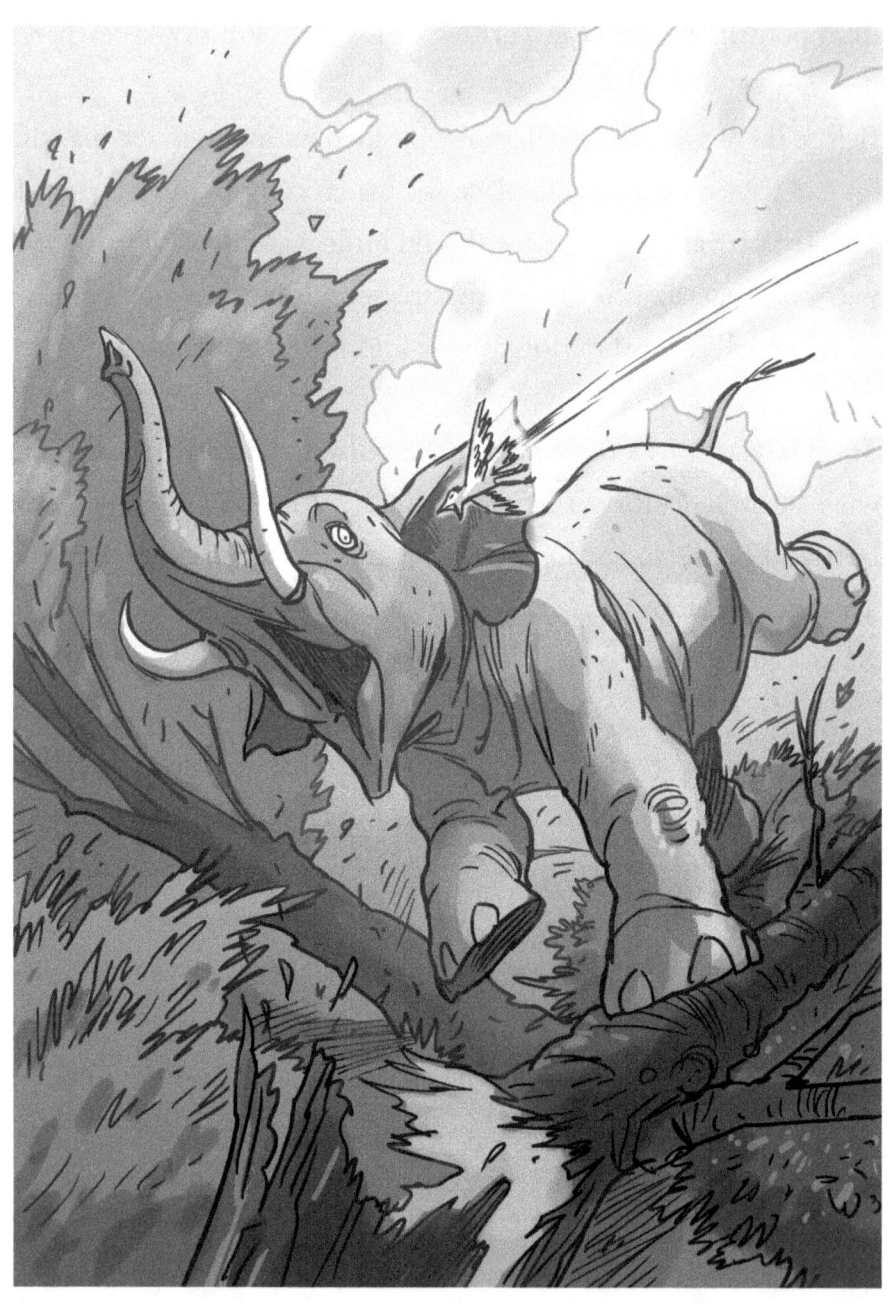

The Elephant and the Hawk
at Daggers Drawn

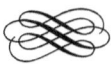

The story of the Elephant and the Hawk in the forest speaks contrary to the idea that might is always right in conflict resolution. In fact, wisdom is more powerful than anything.

Once upon a time, in the forest where they both lived, the Elephant used his large size and destroyed the eggs of the Hawk. During one of his routine walks looking for food, the Ezlephant mistakenly slammed into one of the trees in which the Hawk had laid her eggs. When the nest fell out of the tree, the Elephant smashed the nest unconsciously. The Hawk was away that day too, looking for food, so, by the time the Hawk returned, she could not find her home.

When she noticed that the elephant had trampled on it she was very angry and screamed, "What has this Elephant with his big feet done to me? Look at my nest and the eggs destroyed by him! This is terrible. I must ask him why he did this because enough is enough."

The Hawk flew around to look for the Elephant and suddenly spotted him about one mile away from the nest. So, the Hawk flew by and perched on the tree near the Elephant. She then approached the Elephant angrily,

"Hey you! Why did you destroy my nest and eggs? Are you jealous of me? You think your size can frighten me? You are callous. This is not right."

The Elephant arrogantly turned his back to the Bird and spoke to her,

"Who are you? Stop disturbing me. I have had a very long and tiring day. If you bother me again, I will kill you right now. Why did you lay eggs in a tree in the first place? You cannot blame me for an accident that was unintended. Leave now or else I will kill you and eat you.Hahahahahahahaha, poor Hawk, there is nothing you can do. You may lick your wounds and take your leave."

The Hawk was really afraid of being killed because the Elephant was huge and could trap the Hawk with his trunk, wrap it around her and swallow her in two minutes. So, the disgusted Hawk flew further away from the Elephant and responded to his threats only when she was very sure of her safety. Then the Hawk said,

"We shall see who is who in this forest. I expected you to be sorry and apologize for hurting me, but you are boasting with your size and threatening to kill me. I must retaliate."

The Elephant turned and laughed, "Hahahahahaha, you little helpless Hawk! How will you retaliate when you cannot even stand near me to talk to me? Why are you far away from me? Come closer and repeat what you are saying so I can kill you. Hahahahahahahaha, don't make a fool of yourself in front of anyone in this forest by saying that you want to retaliate against me because my name is Elephant and not Hawk."

The Hawk was disappointed, frustrated and angry because the Elephant did not care about her feelings. She left the scene but it would not take long for the Elephant to discover that he was living in a world of false assumptions.

The Elephant was convinced that the problem was over but it was an illusion because the Hawk was going to retaliate. When she could not get the Elephant to talk amicably, she decided to complain to the other birds in the forest, but none of them could even fly near the Elephant because of his ability to use his long trunk to catch anything around him.

It seemed at that point that the Hawk's case was closed but she never gave up. She withdrew for a while and began thinking creatively. After studying the size of the Elephant and his movement, the

Hawk quickly noticed that there was a weakness from which she could attack him successfully and subdue him without being killed. That weakness was the Elephant's large ear with its wide opening. The Hawk felt optimistic and said,

"I will fly up into the sky and then dive into the large ear of the Elephant and stay there as long as I want. This will really be uncomfortable for him. In that way he will be restless and weary until he will pass out. I will make sure that I don't come out of his ear until he is completely subdued by my action. I know he will not identify me."

The Hawk knew it was time for her to execute her plans. When the moment came she never hesitated. She flew right into the ear of the Elephant and created an inconvenient presence there. She held the Elephant captive and disturbed him as she constantly played inside his ear drum causing total discomfort and great pain. He was much traumatized and began to scream for help.

"Oh, God, what is happening in my ear? I have been hearing some unusual noises made by an unwanted object. I don't know what is going on. I wonder if the Hawk is doing this to me. Hawk, are you the one inside my ear? Come out immediately!"

The Elephant was traumatized and outraged. He beat himself about the bush, struggling to get rid of the mysterious presence inside his ear but he could not. As he became unsettled, it was evident because the trees and the grass suffered at his hands. While all the animals and birds nearby watched, the Elephant gradually collapsed. It was not long before he died as a result of fatigue from the struggle.

The onlookers were shocked. As they went closer to investigate what could have happened, to their great shock, the Hawk flew out of the Elephant's ear and up to a nearby tree where she posted her grievance to the assembly of the animals and birds.

The Hawk said, "I know all of you are shocked but that Elephant lying there dead destroyed my nest with my eggs inside it. When and I asked him why he did that to me, he threatened to kill me. As a result, I decided to seek justice. I wanted to prove to the Elephant that his size did not matter."

The Lion, Tiger and Baboon were present, but it was the Lion, who roared and said, "You little bird, what did you just do to one of us? You will be arrested and charged in the court of the animals for murder of the Elephant. I am the King of the Jungle. Why did you not come to me to report the matter?"

The Hawk responded to the Lion, "I don't trust you because you have been killing other small animals in this forest. This has caused some of them to be afraid of you. Do you notice that when you are around, they always run into hiding?"

The Lion roared angrily, "That is not your business! Never mind that. I have to kill some of the animals and eat when I am hungry. How could a small bird like you dare to kill the big Elephant? You need to be stopped because you are a threat to the family of animals in this forest, you little bird."

The Hawk responded, "Hahahahahahaha, your size is nothing of concern to me. I am no longer afraid of any animal. I will deal with all of you because I have wings to fly but you don't."

The Lion and the other animals were furious when they heard this. The Lion roared again and jumped up into the sky in an attempt to grab the Hawk but he could not jump high enough.

Since the Lion was King of the Jungle, he ordered the Tiger and the Baboon to arrest the Hawk and all other birds nearby. As they tried to arrest them all of the birds flew away up into the sky, laughing. The Lion and the other animals were very disappointed. They regretted the death of the Elephant and wished they had intervened earlier to prevent and resolve the conflict.

This was not a happy ending for anyone.

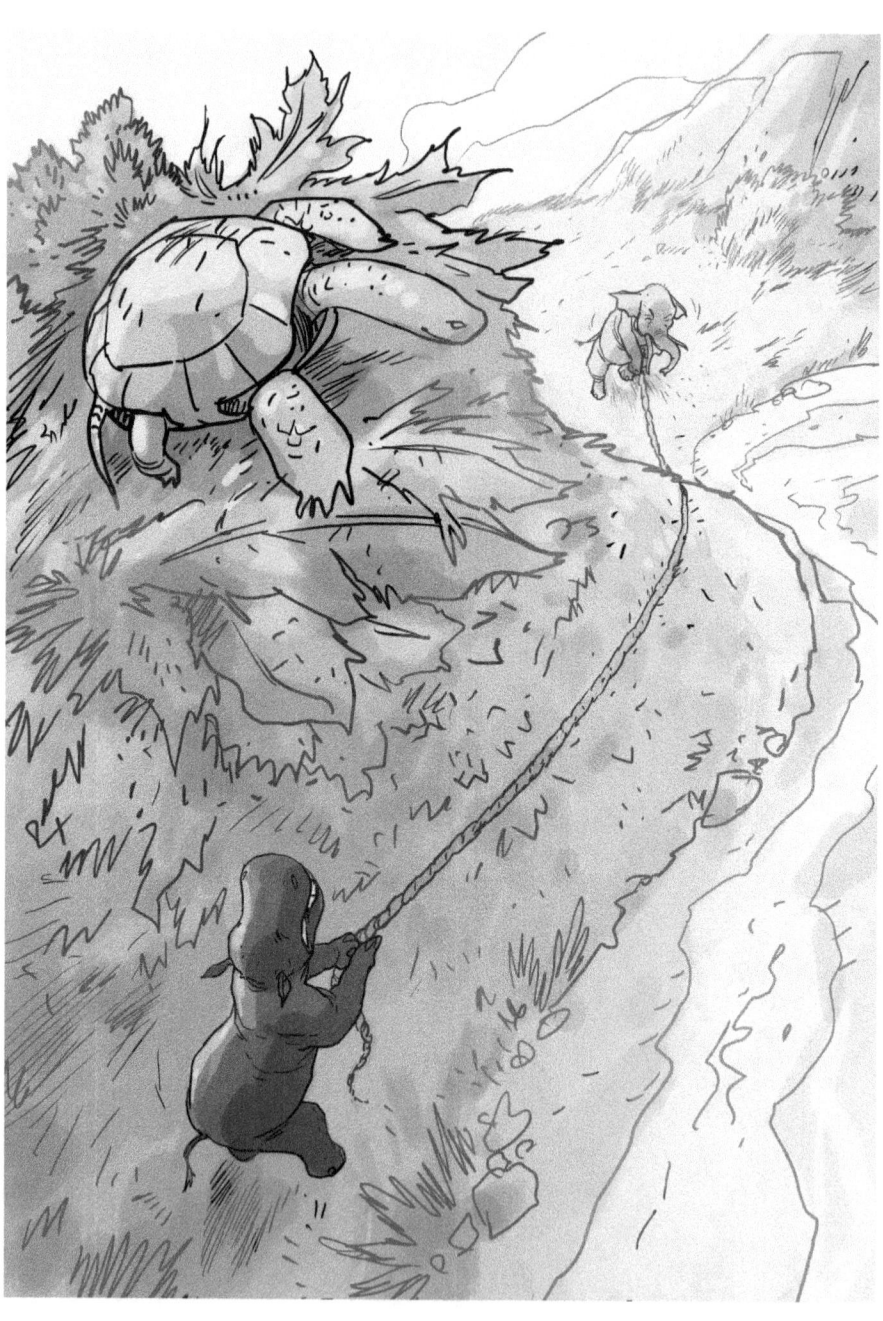

The Tortoise's Tug of War with the Elephant and Hippopotamus

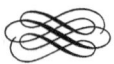

The Tortoise lived near the river at the bottom of the mountain that stretched across to the vast forest deserted by humans and only used occasionally for hunting. The Tortoise inhabited only a small portion of the forest. He was disgruntled because he did not have enough space for himself and he was tired of the obnoxious and superimposing presence of both the Elephant, who occupied a larger portion of the forest, and the Hippopotamus, who inhabited the river valley. Imagine what the Tortoise had to put up with living near these two supersized animals every single day of his life! One day when the Tortoise was really upset he said,

"I am really sick and tired of the presence of the Elephant and Hippo in this forest and valley. I can't have a peaceful sleep and this has been going on for more than fifty years now. They are too loud and too noisy both during the day and the night. Besides, they are occupying too much land for themselves. I think I need to ask for the forest and valley to be shared equally. It might help to reduce the disturbance if I acquire more land. I will try to contact them separately to discuss a plan and hopefully they will agree to my proposition."

It was extremely annoying for the small tortoise who preferred a quiet and peaceful environment for himself. To make matters worse, both the Elephant and Hippo would never cooperate with the small Tortoise. Yet, the Tortoise was never afraid to call them to order. In his latest grievance, posted to the Elephant separately he wrote,

"Dear Elephant, I urge you to maintain some peace and order in this forest at night in order for me and my family to sleep peacefully. You are too loud and noisy. You should respect my right to live in this forest. I also want the forest to be shared equally between you and me." The Elephant read the notice and responded angrily,

"Tortoise, look here. Never bother me again with your stupid demands. I am not going to be quiet. If you don't like it here, you can pack and leave. I am the Elephant and I won't share this forest with a small Tortoise like you. Only the King of the Jungle can cause me to listen. So don't disturb me again or else I will kick you out of this forest."

Then the Tortoise went over to the valley and posted another grievance to the Hippo by writing this,

"Dear Hippo, you are too noisy at night and it is distracting me from a sound sleep. Please, stop your activities at night so that I can sleep quietly and peacefully. You know I have to wake up early in the morning to go to work, and it is not fair that you continue to be mischievous. I would like to share the valley equally between us. You cannot have the whole valley for yourself alone."

The Hippo read the notice posted by the Tortoise and asked,"What? Who are you, tiny Tortoise, asking me to be quiet? Aren't you afraid of me? I can drag you into this river and drown you. You are crazy to ask me to share the valley with you."

The Tortoise received both responses separately but was alarmed at the threats and lack of cooperation from both the Elephant and the Hippo. He felt bullied and intimidated, but that did not stop him from his quest to make sure that his neighbors were conscious of the law of equality regardless of his size. He thought of a way to get them to cooperate with him. In that way, the three of them with their families could live side-by-side in peace and harmony.

His peace efforts were in vain as the Elephant and Hippopotamus quickly brushed him aside and continued to live as it pleased both of them. Now the Tortoise became increasingly uncomfortable with them but instead of simply moving on, that is packing his things and quitting (which is the normal thing to do for most people who can't stand the might of their opponents), he decided to embark on a dangerous scheme of retaliation. The Tortoise said to himself,

"I plan to have a tug of war with the Elephant and Hippo but I will not talk to them together. I will approach each of them separately. According to the plan, whoever wins will inherit the land while the loser must leave immediately. Now, I will secretly meet separately with the Elephant and the Tortoise. I am ready to overthrow them provided this tug of war plan is successful."

So, the Tortoise put his plans into motion. In those days, tugs of war were very serious and risky because participants were forfeiting their rights to any appeal should they be defeated in such a venture. But it did not bother either the Elephant or the Hippo because both of them felt strongly that each of them was in a position to defeat the small tortoise in any competition, especially in a tug of war. The Tortoise met with the Elephant and said,"Mr. Elephant, I have an idea."

"The Elephant replied, "Are you here to bother me again with your useless demands?"

"No," said the Tortoise. "I want to summon you to a tug of war because you are too mouthy, and I need to prove to you that I am not weak as you think. If I win, you will pack and leave."

"Hahahahahah!" laughed the Elephant. "A tug of war with you? Do you want to be killed even before it has started?"

The Tortoise replied, "I am not afraid. We should compete tomorrow at 5.00 PM."

The Elephant agreed, "Yes, but you will regret it."

Then the Tortoise left and snuck into the valley and met with the Hippo, in his home.

"Mr. Hippo, I have an idea."

The Hippo turned and stared at the Tortoise and responded, "Why do you think only your own ideas are the best? What idea do you have for me, small Tortoise?"

The Tortoise responded, "I want you and me to have a tug of war. Whoever wins will own this whole land. If I will win, you will pack and leave the valley to me."

The Hippo was laughing, "Hahahahahaha, that is not going to happen."

Tortoise insisted and asked again, "Do you agree to the tug of war? It is planned to take place tomorrow at 5.00 PM. Only the tug of war will determine if you are going to continue living here."

Hippo quickly responded, "Ok, ok, Mr. Small Tortoise. Whatever. I will see you tomorrow at 5.00 PM for the tug of war."

The Tortoise walked away laughing to himself, "Yes, yes, I have got them both! Tomorrow at 5.00 PM I will position myself on the mountain top where I will look down on opposite sides to see each of them. But it will be impossible for them to see each other because the mountain will be between them. During the tug of war, I will hide on the mountain top and send the opposite ends of the long, big rope to each of them. Next, I will pull the rope from the center to indicate that the tug of war has started, but the Hippo and the Elephant will be pulling each other without knowing that they have been tricked by me."

From this strategic position the tortoise relaxed as he watched the Elephant and Hippo pull and pull each other in the tug of war non-stop until both of them collapsed.

Laughing at their foolishness the Tortoise crawled down from the mountain top to discover that the Elephant and Hippo had not just collapsed. Both of them were dead! "Hahahahahahahahah!" he laughed as he celebrated and claimed the whole land for himself.

Questions for reflection and discussion

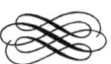

Dear readers,

Thank you for reading these fables. Here are some questions for your reflection and discussion in your groups, communities and societies about the legal, moral and ethical issues evoked in the stories. It will be appreciated if we all have an honest conversation about these issues. Please, feel free to share your thoughts and feelings objectively because the goal is to allow us explore intelligent ways to assert common principles by which we live as well as ascertain the beauty in our differences in this post-modern world also known as global village.

1) When have you acted like a character in these stories? Share your experience.
2) Do you admire any character in the stories? Why?
3) What lessons have you learned from these moral fables in regard to what is happening in our communities, society and world today? What should be done differently in order for people to live in peace and harmony?

4) Why did the Tortoise ask the Lion to jump back into the hole when he knew he would not be rescued again?

5) Why is the Monkey so gracious and kind?

6) Why does the Monkey stop to help the Lion when he knew the lion could hurt him?

7) Why does the Tortoise think that he must be part of the party to the Moon?

8) Why does the Birds invite the Tortoise when they know he was not meant to fly?

(9) According to the story why should the Tortoise be blamed for the demise of the Lion?

10) Why does the Tortoise think he is entitled to the valley?

11) What is your ideal means in resolving personal conflict, interpersonal conflict, intergroup conflict and socio-cultural conflict according to your tradition, culture or religious faith? Let us be bold to confront this issue with regards to the nature and scope of racial and ethnic conflicts both locally and internationally across communities, cities and nations?

12) What have these stories taught you about selfless and heartless pursuits in life?

13) Under what circumstance is turning the other cheek a viable option for conflict resolution?

Jonathan F. Awasom is a voice for the voiceless trapped under oppressive societies in the world. He has spoken truth against abuse of human rights, corporate corruption, genocides, civil wars, human trafficking and the exploitation of powerless people in Africa especially children and women. He was born and raised in Cameroon, West Africa, and through his faith in God he became a passionate advocate for the downtrodden. His work as a civil and human rights advocate has been featured in major newspapers such as the Star Tribune, the Chanhassen and Eden Prairie Newspapers in Minnesota and the Star Ledger in New Jersey. He was educated at the Presbyterian Primary School- Alabukam, Presbyterian Secondary School-Mankon, Government High School-Mbengwi and the Protestant Faculty of Theology in Yaoundé, Cameroon. After moving to the USA he furthered his education at the United Theological Seminary in Minnesota. He holds a Master of Arts in Religion and Theology with concentration in Ethics, Peace and Global Justice. Since then he has participated in different non-degree programs in Non-Profit Ethics and Conflict Resolution under Hamline University in Minnesota. He has trained under the Tentmakers Young Leaders Development Program in Duluth, Minnesota and is also a trained Global Career Development Facilitator (GCDF). He currently lives in New Jersey and loves volunteering for charities such as Habitat for Humanity, Midnight Run, and local soup kitchens. He has worked as a chaplain, youth director, community leader and organizer for different non-profits. He has recently served as a campaign leader and professional fund-raiser for World Vision. He is a World Vision Child Ambassador and is currently pursuing a Master's degree in Organizational Leadership. He believes that we can transform the world to become virtuous and free by breaking down cultural barriers through strategic bridge-building to embrace one another regardless of race, religion, gender or national origin.

TESTIMONIAL AND PHILANTROPIC PURPOSE OF THIS BOOK

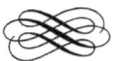

At least 50% of my tuition as a student in a Christian grammar school in Cameroon, Africa, was made possible through a sponsorship program. I would not have been able to afford the cost of education without that extra help. My life has changed because of the power of God's love through giving. I am grateful and would like to give back as a continuous celebration of the human spirit of friendship, kindness, generosity and compassion which have impacted my life educationally. Proceeds from sales of this book will be invested in education, health, nutrition and other sustainable programs, which will help to empower children and their families living under poverty and oppression around the world. Thank you for your support.

Jonathan

Phone: 201-878-5829
Email: Jonathan_light2000@yahoo.com